BOLD LOVE

A Letter to My Young Sisters

Terri M. Bolds, MS, LPC

Copyright © 2016 by Terri M. Bolds
All rights reserved.
Printed and Bound in the United States

Published by
Bold Visions Consulting
(513) 299-8177
www.boldvisionsconsulting.com

Cover Illustration: Mike D. Gray
Cover & Interior Design: TWA Solutions.com

Second Printing: May 2019
ISBN: 978-1-7330563-0-4

All rights reserved. No part of this book may be reproduced, stored in a retrieval system or transmitted in any form or by any means without the prior written permission of the publisher—except by a reviewer who may quote brief passages in a review to be printed in a newspaper, magazine or journal.

For inquiries, speaking engagements, book signings, literary events, contact: boldcounselor3@gmail.com.

Dedication

To my parents, thank you for giving me life.

Mommy, thank you for everything.

To my three sets of grandparents, your love has carried me through life.

To my siblings, you'll always have my heart.

To the Bolds, Clingman and Denton families, thank you.

To my forever friends, your love is invaluable.

To that special someone, thank you for sticking by me through this process.

To the men and women that took it upon themselves to love and mentor me, thank you.

To my former educators that still teach and support me beyond your responsibility, thank you.

God, for all the above it is you that I owe my life and deepest gratitude.

TABLE OF CONTENTS

Foreword 7

Introduction 9

Ugly 13

Chapter 1: Our Minds 15

Chapter 2: Maslow's Theory 24

Chapter 3: Learned Behavior 30

Chapter 4: Daddy Woes 35

Daddy's Girl 45

Chapter 5: Worthy 47

Melanin Me.. 52

Conclusion 54

About the Author... 59

FOREWORD

Bold Love: A Letter to My Young Sisters delivers an entertaining and realistic perspective of the struggles of African American girls as they develop self-identify and self-esteem. It addresses a personal perspective to build awareness on how women identify and define beauty.

Terri M. Bolds shares personal struggles that provide the reader an opportunity to establish a personal connection with her. Not only does she explore the history of the role of women, she pulls that historical aspect and current role of women in today's reality. Terri utilizes personal and professional background to address self-esteem using a cognitive behavioral approach. She shares how her multifaceted background establishes her expertise in the area of mental health, and her strategic understanding of the mental process that take place with the topic at hand.

Terri also explores and defines how that theoretical approach can be used to make sense of the thought process when defining beauty. *Bold Love: A Letter to My Young Sisters* also explores the father-daughter relationship, and the effects of an absent father, as it is not an unknown factor, especially in the African American home. The book addresses the emotional effect on a young girl. It takes a unique approach of correlation of the love of God and loving yourself as parallel with healthy self-identify. Addressing the fact that we are loved by God and He made us in His likeness, and how learning self-worth are key components to healthy self-esteem and self-identity.

— Kachanda Hewitt, MS

INTRODUCTION

Dear Black Girl,

My journey is worth journaling and one that I believe can help someone else. Learning to love myself is a continuous process, and I humbly welcome the growth that has taken place. Humbled because there was a time when I thought that to look at me was to see a fat, unhappy, girl with two birth defects on her face, also known as dimples. Humbled because I did not let the taunts about my weight or the fullness of my lips tear me down to the point of no return. Humbled that despite what seemed to be a life story chronicling dejection and self-hatred, I am a survivor of my own mind. I made the choice to release the negative thoughts that had plagued the mind and soul of a young woman who was yearning to feel normal. My journey is one that I was too shy and embarrassed to discuss: I have come from the absence of a parent, sexual abuse, being talked about, wondering why the boys did not like me, and hopelessly gazing at my friends and others that I felt had better lives than mine.

But God…I am thankful for a God who thought enough of me to intentionally show me my worth, beauty, and purpose. There is a song by CeCe Winans that simply says, "Mercy said no." Mercy decided my life was worth more than the pain, and shame that I carried with me. Mercy is that by which my life is saved daily and refuses to let me go. Grace and Mercy saved my life and provided new experiences. Mercy decided that I am worthy. Mercy decided I get another chance, and Mercy said "Release your fears! And oh, but what about Grace? Grace, the precious gift that keeps on giving, teaches me humility and gratitude for all things. Mercy: not receiving the punishment I deserve. Grace: unmerited favor. Because God, my higher power (yours may be something else), decided I was worthy and because I listened, I am here, a brand new me to share some words of wisdom with my young sisters of color.

Growing up as a black female carries a weight greater than most can understand. History tells a story of the woman being the rock of families. The woman is hard-working, provides for her family, is submissive yet strong--the Proverbs 31 woman. As society has evolved, our image of the black woman has changed. The woman has worked in the civil rights movement, been a flower child, learned the latest dance steps. She has justified why she has been seen in compromising positions on social media, has been depicted as backbiting her friends, accepting disrespect from men, and has been degraded by a commerce that profits from portraying embarrassing trends. So how can growing up as a black girl be an easy or even understandable task? Who are we supposed to be? The girl who accepts a man who blatantly disrespects his responsibilities (Know that being a girl who disrespects the black man and fails to uphold her responsibilities is shameful too), or the girl who upholds a moral standard and is therefore viewed as lame?

Deciding the type of black girl you want to be is all up to you, just as it is up to me regarding who I want to be. No one else can make the decision of how we choose to leave our mark on this planet. Sure, our families, friends, society, and environment are influential, but the choice is yours and mine.

Through this body of writing, sage for my black sisters, my hope is to encourage the ability to view oneself as worthy of love, worthy of success, worthy of accepting how we were created, and worthy of life. The following is written for encouragement and normalcy. Included are quotations from women about their experiences with self-love, poems, and a first-person narrative. This letter is intended to be a teaching tool.

Ugly

By Terri M. Bolds

Have you ever felt so ugly you asked God why?
Why didn't you care enough about me to make me thin,
Or narrow my nose, or lengthen my hair or why did you think it
Was ok that I have lips so full that no matter what I do or don't do I look like
A character in a minstrel show?
Have you ever felt so ugly that when you look in the mirror you see another person,
An image of the vision you believe God should have had when he created you,
An image that you are sure would cause you less heartache, less stress and more contentment?
Have you ever felt so ugly you search and search for ways to disappear,
Ways to seem invisible
Ways to hide your ugly?
Have you ever felt so ugly that you look at your friends with envy?
God liked them more. He liked them more because they have crushes that crush back
They can't fit their mothers' clothes, the cascading hair, people listen to them, and they are pretty and well,
You're ugly
Have you ever thought am I really ugly, or a reflection of the hurt that I have built up and stored

And allowed to saturate my mind, my body, my every being,
Or that perhaps the vision you see is a reflection of God, and if so, ugly? Can you really be?
Because how can a reflection of the Great I Am, the one that created the land and stars, the one whose words parted the Red Sea, be the same one that created me, an ugly me.
Me, a reflection of Him and Him of me, and me of Him and Him of me
So perhaps that image of ugly that I see is not me. Because in order for me to be ugly, that means a flaw in his creation of me, the me that he purposed me to be. Not the me that looks with envy, not the me that feels cheated, not the me that feels ugly but the me that was created purposely and purposeful,
Because I am a reflection of Him and He of me

CHAPTER 1

Our Minds

As a licensed mental health counselor, I work from a cognitive behavioral mindset. "Behavioral and Cognitive Psychology is a specialty in professional psychology that reflects an experimental clinical approach distinguished by the use of principles of human learning and development and theories of cognitive processing to promote meaningful change in maladaptive human behavior and thinking"(American Psychological Association, 2016). Plainly stated, our thoughts are linked to our behavior. The illustration that I use to visually explain this school of thought is:

COGNITIVE BEHAVIORAL THEORY

TRIGGERS ➡ THOUGHTS ➡ BEHAVIORS ➡ CONSEQUENCES

(EVENTS)　　(EMOTIONS)　　　　　　　(NEGATIVE OR POSITIVE)

Basically, we are a people who function as this flow chart so depicts. Think about a situation in your life and plug it into the illustration. For example, my grandmother died, I blamed God, so I stopped going to church, and as I grew in my knowledge that was a negative consequence for me. By the way, consequence is simply the outcome, or result, not just having a negative connotation. Different events in our lives lead to some kind of feeling or thought about the event, and then we respond accordingly. Many of my life's consequences or outcomes are largely a direct correlation to my life's experiences. With years of holding onto hurt, hopes and promises unfilled and loss, I was captive to my own irrational thinking. The thinking was irrational because I had an "all or nothing" perspective or "unsubstantiated truths" that fueled my existence. My relationship with my father is estranged, so why would any other man want me, for example, or I have to be perfect in order for people to love me. All of those thoughts and feelings were so heavy and plaguing to the point of leading to my first seizure. I believe God was telling me that I could not be all things to all people, and that it is okay for me to take care of myself. He slowed me down and still does to this day, 11 years after my first seizure. Grace and Mercy.

When I think about my life, and the decisions I made, I realize my view was foggy. Now, my view is one with more clarity, understanding, and compassion. The prisms of my mind bogged me down with the thought that no one would miss me at the age of 14 when I contemplated suicide. It was not until I became more knowledgeable on the topic that I later understood I was dealing with adjustment challenges: my grandmother died and I started high school, all of which were major life changes. I was plagued with thoughts of being "unpretty." It was easier not to express interest in boys because they were not expressing interest in me. All the while, deep inside, I envied the girls who were dating, writing notes, and sneaking out of the house to see their boyfriends. I often fixated on the notion that it was because of my full-figured frame, pink full lips and nerdiness that no one wanted me. Naturally, I attempted to change myself for attention; I tried ridiculous diets, new hairstyles, fashion and even dummying myself. I fit right in to TLC's song titled Unpretty: which describes the life of one that attempted to fit in by changing their hair or buying the latest makeup, but without loving what's within, there is no point in doing all of those other things, because what's inside will always radiate. At some point the fake "you" will not be enough to mask how you really are and how you really feel on the inside.

Literally, take a look in the mirror. Sometimes, that simple task is not so simple. Take a look at the person looking back at you and be honest about what you see. If you see a negative depiction, write that down. If you see vanity, if you see fear, hate, love, despair, whatever you see, write those things down and begin to make yourself your personal project. You're the most important project to date. Begin to pick yourself apart. There is one key element that has to be a part of the process: honesty. I once heard a facilitator in a workshop on addictions say that you have to get "butt naked honest" to uncover all those layers down to the core. Mental health is often associated with being "crazy" rather than experiencing any of the following:

- Grief
- Inadequacy
- Dysfunctional relationships
- Happiness
- Sadness
- Low and high self-esteem
- Fear

In order to fully address the mental health needs of an individual, a systemic approach, an approach that addresses the whole individual, can be proven to be more effective than addressing one issue. Systems Therapy can be applied to organizations, couples, communities, or families. The technique relies on identifying specific behavior patterns and noting how each member responds to anxiety within the dynamic. By doing this, the individual participants can begin to understand and transform their patterns to more adaptive, productive behaviors" (grouptherapy.com, 2013). Once an individual becomes in tune with his/her cognitions, behavioral patterns and how they correlate with their interaction toward society, then one may begin to work on eradicating maladaptive interactions that limit healthy functioning.

So, take some time, come back if you need to but answer these questions:

- Do I like myself?

_____
_____
_____
_____
_____
_____
_____
_____
_____

- Why do I like myself or why do I not like myself?

_____
_____
_____
_____
_____
_____
_____
_____

- Do others like me?

  _____
  _____
  _____
  _____
  _____
  _____
  _____
  _____
  _____

- Do people love me?

  _____
  _____
  _____
  _____
  _____
  _____
  _____
  _____
  _____
  _____

Bold Love: A Letter To My Young Sisters

- What is my definition of love?

  _____
  _____
  _____
  _____
  _____
  _____
  _____
  _____

- How do I know if people love me?

  _____
  _____
  _____
  _____
  _____
  _____
  _____
  _____

- How would I honestly describe myself?

_____
_____
_____
_____
_____
_____
_____
_____

- Are there things I would like to change about me?

_____
_____
_____
_____
_____
_____
_____
_____

Testimonial

"Many kids experienced being the "fat" kid growing up, but it was the opposite for me. I was that really skinny kid struggling to fit into my body and a new culture. I remember trying to wear tights and socks that were baggy on me- being called "African Booty Scratcher" (sic) and "Somali" [mocking the starving refugees]. I even took weight gain shakes and protein drinks to help me gain weight. BUT today through God's Grace and a circle of friends that have become my family I am doing just fine on a lot of levels. After having my almost 11 pound son at 30- I have healthy weight to work off and refine my body."

– *Anonymous, Age 35*

CHAPTER 2

Maslow's Theory

How many times have you heard someone or you yourself have said, "I don't need nobody", "Just me myself and I", "I can protect myself", "I don't need to feel important"? Lies!!

Self-actualization
personal growth and fulfilment

Esteem needs
achievement, status, responsibility, reputation

Belongingness and Love needs
family, affection, relationships, work group, etc.

Safety needs
protection, security, order, law, limits, stability, etc.

Biological and Physiological needs
basic life needs - air, food, drink, shelter, warmth, sex, sleep, etc.

"Each of us is motivated by needs. Our most basic needs are inborn, having evolved over tens of thousands of years. Abraham Maslow's Hierarchy of Needs helps to explain how these needs motivate us all. Maslow's Hierarchy of Needs states that we must satisfy each need in turn, starting with the first, which deals with the most obvious needs for survival itself. Only when the lower order needs of physical and emotional well-being are satisfied are we concerned with the higher order needs of influence and personal development. Conversely, if the things that satisfy our lower order needs are swept away, we are no longer concerned about the maintenance of our higher order needs", (Abraham Maslow original Hierarchy of Needs concept 1954; Alan Chapman review and other material, design, code 1995-2014).

What this theory basically says is that you need people. Fulfillment and success are things that one cannot accomplish alone. How many times have we been hurt and say things like, "I'm just gone do me," "That's why I don't have friends," or "Family ain't nothing?" That is a cause and effect relationship. We have negative experiences then assume all experiences will be as the previous. We don't realize that generalization can stunt our growth. Sometimes, we cause the continuous effects in our lives and do not take accountability. We do not look at our patterns or learn our thought processes, desires, or needs. Maslow's theory tells us the basic needs of an individual, but how much can we accomplish from the bottom of the hierarchy to the top? If those bottom needs are not met, the others become a broken ladder that needs constant restructuring to reach the top. Ask yourself these questions:

- What are my needs?

- How can others meet my needs?

- How can I help others help me meet my needs?

- How can I deal with disappointment when my needs are not met?

- How do I want to be treated when I mess up?

_____
_____
_____
_____
_____
_____
_____
_____
_____

Testimonial

"Growing up, everyone experiences times where they aren't exactly sure of who they are, what they represent, and where they fit in. I was always a child/teen that had lots of friends, which led to me having an awesome social life. But as exciting as my childhood and adolescent years were and despite how happy and confident I seemed to be on the outside, there was something that was holding me back from showing the world who I really was.

I came from a family that I felt, in comparison to that of my peers, was "different" to say the least. The culture and everyday dynamics of my household were definitely a part of my life that

Bold Love: A Letter To My Young Sisters

I was ashamed of. The religion that we practiced, the language that we spoke at home, all the way to the way that my parents dressed, were details of my life that I kept hidden from my peers. Growing up around so much diversity, I'm not quite sure why I didn't cherish the uniqueness of my upbringing, but I definitely saw it more of a burden than the blessing that it was.

It wasn't until I graduated high school and went on to attend college that I began to take pride in who I really was. I think I can attribute my growth to my being roommates with my best friend/sister/cousin (who was raised the same way) and finally having a peer who shared similar beliefs as I did. We were both away from home, amongst a couple thousand young minds that were all searching for themselves. In college, it's okay to be you, unapologetically. It's a time of discovery, growth as well as reflection. And during my college years, I found the beauty in which I was (sic). And guess what? People loved me and were and still are intrigued by all of my uniqueness."

– **Anonymous, Age 33**

CHAPTER 3

Learned Behavior

"Do as I say, not as I do" is a statement that has been heard throughout black households for years. Cutting a ham to put in the roaster was done because that is what grandma and big mama did, generationally not knowing it was because they did not have a large enough roaster. We got spanked so, of course, we would spank our kids. So many times, the people we become have a direct correlation to where we came from. Not all of our experiences learned have a negative impact on our lives, for example, working hard to get what we want, being respectful, and learning how to cook some good ole soul food. But let's look at some things we may have learned that could have a negative impact on our lives. For example:

- Hustling (street life, drugs, gambling, theft, etc.)

- Bashing men
- Having bad attitudes
- Depending on men or government assistance
- Being irresponsible with money
- Thinking we need to change ourselves to fit in
- Bashing other women
- Keeping harmful family secrets
- Desiring instant gratification

Do you see yourself fitting into any of the above categories? What ideologies have you adopted that may be harmful to your life? All things learned are not damaging, but many times the negative seems to linger longer and smell stronger. At what point do you decide what is right and wrong? Choosing to know better in order to do better helps to break unhealthy cycles of generational trauma and ignorance. At some point, accountability needs to take place in order for growth to take place. Living life riding on the coat tails of resentment ("Well my mama did or my daddy did," or "I didn't have," or "Nobody liked me") will get you nowhere. What will make you soar is how you have overcome. Excuses are not permissible with maturity. Blame is not permissible for survival. Fear is a disaster for a life full of apathy. In order to fulfill our life's purpose we have to take responsibility for ourselves. Truth lives within accountability, and without it you are nothing but an underdeveloped being lacking the proper nourishment to flourish. Dr. Maya Angelou once said, "When someone shows you who they are, believe them the first time." I often ask myself if I want people to believe I am the learned mess that I adopted or awesomeness that was birthed from it.

Testimonial

I remember like it was yesterday. Even though I'm grown now... somethings never leave your memory or your life. At age 7, I wish would banish far from me (sic).

I am a woman who was raped by her father. I don't cry anymore when I say it out loud. But my stomach still drops. I'm 34 now. And my father is up for parole this month for the umpteenth time since he was incarcerated the year I turned 8.

As a child when going through things you don't ask why me,' only when you become an adult you look back and say sheesh... why me. I don't know really how to begin.

I was a regular 7 year old. Mom and dad married. [I] had two younger brothers at the time. My mother was going to school at night for her BS. My father would be at home. And one night he just called me into his room. Asked me to get ready for a bath. I already took my bath, I challenged him. He said it again. This tall man standing 6'4," hovering over me. I wasn't scared I was confused. I always did what I was told. Then he began to touch me. I closed my eyes so tight. I had so many thoughts. I was then scared. Seven years old naked and afraid. Confused of what just happened (sic). Then he told me to go and take a bath. I just remember crying. It happened every night my mother went to class. He threatened to kill my mother if she ever found out. I promised not to tell. I always kept my promises. Because I'm responsible. I'm the eldest. I'm the example. I'm me.

One night I woke up to my mother being punched and dragged across the family room then into the sitting room area. I went to go help but she yelled at me to go back in my room. My father was beating her…I thought she found out and he was going to kill her.

It went on forever it felt like. I finally heard the police. I opened my door slowly and peeked around the door. They questioned my mother [about] what [had] happened. My father left before they arrived. I went back in my room. The police came then knocked on my bedroom door. I opened it and I apologized. Is my mommy dead I asked? The officer told me no. And I just looked for her….she sat on the couch crying and trying to talk at the same time. I'll never forget her voice at that time. I tried to climb in her lap but she said it hurt. So I got down and stood there. Looking. Hopeless. A day later she came to me and asked me how I was…did I want to talk to her about anything. I asked her is he coming back. She said no. Do I have to see him again…

she looked perplexed and said not if you don't want to...she said what's wrong...I started to cry. I told her everything.

The next day I went to the doctor. Then to counseling then to more counseling...then to trial. To testify against my father. This was extremely scary. I'm 8 now. And I have an understanding that my father is ill. And it shouldn't have happened to me. But it did. And now he is going to prison and I have to be apart. Eighteen to life he has to serve, without parole. He is up now for parole because the last two years he has been seeing a therapist and he has sickle cell. So he is sick. And wants out of prison.

I'm a whole person and sharing is healing me. I'm not damaged. Just lived a lot of life at a terrible young age (sic).

– Anonymous, Age 34

CHAPTER 4

Daddy Woes

Imagine being a little girl watching other little girls with their fathers, sometimes in her own family and constantly feeling like something is flawed within her because her father is not there. Imagine visiting your father yearly and feeling like you are meeting him over again each time. Imagine Father's Day and you begin to wonder about the type of men those cards, commercials, and movies speak of. Imagine living a fairytale hoping that one day you will have the relationship that you have dreamt of, seen and heard about. Now imagine carrying all of that baggage with you, weighing you down and destroying any relationship that comes in your path. I am here to tell you that is a devastating life and recipe for disaster.

For so many years resentment ruled my thoughts. The absence of a foundational relationship with my father handicapped me for years. I felt as if I were owed an explanation, but instead

I continually received promises delivered by the absent parent and avoidance by the parent who was present in my life. I felt resentment over the fact that I had suffered all my life because I hadn't felt myself worthy of my father's love, attention or concern. I received only child support and Christmas gifts. I felt resentment toward those who dismissed my feelings by making excuses and telling me to turn the other cheek. I felt resentment over the fact that my whole life I had had a struggle with my sense of self-worth and a fear of loss. I was devastated each time a relationship changed in my life.

What is a daddy? A daddy is your father with a personal touch. The man that you seek for acceptance, for love, for protection. A daddy is the intimate relationship with your father that streams beyond his name on your birth certificate. A daddy is the one who endearingly threatens your first date or calls you randomly to see how you are when you are away from home. A daddy is the one man that you know has your best interest at heart. A daddy may not always fit the story book definition, but he fits the bill nonetheless. A daddy is that man that when you see him, your eyes light up and you let the world know, "That's my daddy." Unfortunately, so many black girls lack that relationship with their father.

Growing up, I could count on one hand how many of my friends had active relationships with their fathers or had fathers in the home. As I got older, I wondered why. What is it about black families that lack the presence of the conventional family? That is not to say that other races don't have the same issues or concerns. Many people whom I knew growing up had stepfathers whom they may or may not have liked, fathers whom they loved but did not live with, or fathers whom they hardly saw. In some cases, fathers were present physically but absent emotionally. Even as a young person, I wondered why. Why didn't we all have a Huxtable family? I began to think if you lived with your mother and father, and they were actively a part of your life, you had been specially picked. I thought maybe the family I thought I should have had happened only outside of black neighborhoods because it was so foreign in mine.

With age comes wisdom. The absence of my father has affected my life in a way that I have to fight daily, dismantling self-condemning thoughts. The loss of that relationship and continued disappointment have created a dysfunctional pathology that I have had to consciously make an effort to reverse. Choosing psychology as my major in undergraduate school and mental health counseling in graduate school were turning points in my life. It was at that time that I began to view my situation for what it was and work to moving from victim status to, "This is my reality, but I don't have to like it." Since that time, I have studied and learned this simple thought: you cannot put expectations on people that they are unwilling to or cannot fulfill. That idea has changed my life. I still struggle, but I don't have daddy woes anymore.

I don't let people discount me, and I don't take their advice to turn the other cheek in order for me to continue subjecting my feelings to situations that repeatedly tear me down. For me, growth and wisdom have come from understanding that we all have a past that affects our future. When we don't address the hurt, neglect, fear, loss, and abuse of our pasts we then create a continuous cycle. A cycle that can systematically tear a legacy down if no one admits the truth and executes change. My parents have a past that they carry with them, and I cannot fault them for how they dealt with situations in their lives. Yes, I have had a rough time, but grace and mercy set me free. I began to insert change in my communications with them. Sometimes patterns change and sometimes they don't, but my responsibility is to myself and to exercising my control over situations. My parents gave me life, and for that they will always have my heart. For their hurts, hard work, love, and struggle, I will forever be grateful. To my mother, for allowing me to live the life she so passionately believed I would succeed in, I am grateful. For the choice to have me when she was young and guide me in a caring and passionate way, I'm grateful. For telling me college was not a choice but was where I was going whether I liked it or not, I'm grateful.

Sometimes we dwell so heavily on what we don't have, we overlook our blessings. The negative has a way of beaming our hurts through every sky we see, in every song we hear, and article we read. Not having my father as an active force in my life was not a punishment or a death sentence and it is not for others either. Take a minute and reflect over your life and think about these things:

- Was I being saved from something?

　

- Is my life a total failure? (BE HONEST, NOT VICTIMIZED)

- Who was with me along the way?

_____
_____
_____
_____
_____
_____
_____

- What lessons have I learned?

_____
_____
_____
_____
_____
_____
_____
_____

- How has this situation shaped me?

_____
_____
_____
_____
_____
_____
_____
_____

- Who was with me who didn't have to be?

_____
_____
_____
_____
_____
_____
_____
_____

- Who loved me when I didn't feel worthy?

_____
_____
_____
_____
_____
_____
_____
_____
_____

It was not until college that I had a "WOW" moment. All that time I felt sorry for myself due to focusing on what I didn't have or thought I should have, when all the time it was presented in other forms. I can honestly say the people in my life are a reminder of God's grace over my life. A spiritual father, that not only was the first person I learned about God from, baptized me and loved me, but a man who told me he would be honored for me to call him dad. He told me that he takes that title seriously, and that I am worthy of the title daughter. There are not enough words in the English language to describe how I still feel to this day when I think about that very special moment. Then there is another man whom many thought was my father because of his presence, a man whom my friends and family are very familiar with. Out of thousands and thousands of people I spotted waving trying to get my attention during my college graduation, he greeted me with a loud, "AYE GIRL," as I so anxiously approached my loved ones after my graduate school graduation. He was the one who took me driving, the one who drove an hour to make sure I had food, and the one who was my biggest inspiration to revisit the idea of church. I could go on and on, but it is because of the unconventional fathers in my life that I have had and still have hope in the relationship between a father and daughter: remember, the absence of a relationship is not the absence of you.

Testimonials

For years I didn't know who I was. Searching for happiness through men, troubled relationships, and pressure from those around me, I crashed and burned. Never thinking I was good enough, I turned to love for the answer. Pouring my heart into boyfriends and those I thought cared about me, I tried my hardest to fill my voids with their love. But when they would leave me, I just felt empty again. Now I'm working to fill those empty holes myself so I can completely be whole...myself.

— Anonymous Age 22

***

Terri M. Bolds, MS, LPC

When I was younger I had a lot of self-esteem issues related to my looks and confidence. Even though I was surrounded by people who told me that I could do anything, I didn't believe it for myself. I believed that I wasn't pretty enough, skinny enough, smart enough, or talented enough. On top of that, I was a people pleaser. I wanted people to like what I did or said. It led to me being shy and not putting myself out to take advantage of opportunities.

Now, I have spent time getting over those issues and am in a much better place in life. I am confident in who I am and my abilities. I have realized that the only person I can change is me and if there is something I don't like about me then I need to work on that. I really like who I am!

—Anonymous, Age 44

Daddy's Girl

By Terri M. Bolds

Daddy? You have one, where did you get him from?

Do they have more? Can you share yours?

But why not me, was I not smart enough, was I not pretty enough or was I not man enough?

Daddy? He plays with you? He tells you he loves you?

Tell me more, because only in my dreams do I have a daddy

A daddy that tells me I'm beautiful, a daddy that tells me he won't let anyone harm me, a daddy that loves me.

Why don't I have a daddy? What did I do? Oh wait, I see you, but you are so far from me…

The promises have jaded my mind and trickled over into all mankind

Tell me, why would he love me when my daddy don't, why would he be true when my daddy won't

I'm not pretty cause my daddy never said so, I'm not smart because my daddy never said so, I'm not worthy because my daddy, wait, where did he go?

Terri M. Bolds, MS, LPC

Oh there you go, you go again and again. Why don't you stay? Daddy what did I do? Daddy… can I call you daddy, I'm not sure, wait where did you go?

Daddy, I'm sorry but I get it now

You couldn't be what I needed you to be, but you created me so because of you I am me.

I wish that more of you, was the Daddy I needed you to be, but Daddy, I'm free

Free from the hurt, shame, anger, the disappointment,

But Daddy there is still some sadness, but Daddy it's ok

It took some time but I learned I am worthy even though you didn't see me

Daddy it's ok, I had those that loved me and still nurture me.

So daddy, it's ok, ease your mind because I am loving the me that I fought so hard to be

I missed out on being Daddy's girl, but love didn't skip me.

So thank you Daddy, for creating me, the me that I now see is still fighting to stay free.

Daddy, you don't have to leave, but know I am a mature me. Daddy's girl has grown up but you can still

Come grow with and get to know me.

CHAPTER 5

Worthy

"Who taught you to hate the color of your skin? Who taught you to hate the texture of your hair? Who taught you to hate the shape of your nose and the shape of your lips? Who taught you to hate yourself from the top of your head to the soles of your feet? Who taught you to hate your own kind? Who taught you to hate the race that you belong to so much so that you don't want to be around each other? You should ask yourself who taught you to hate being what God made you." Words from Malcolm X. These words were spoken in 1962, but they could not be more relevant in 2016. Being a black woman in America comes with heavy weight, not only are our experiences different, but we look different. In a society where implants, Botox, injections and make up "beats" are the entire rave, there is a culture fighting to make its presence to increase self-love.

Terri M. Bolds, MS, LPC

When I look at media publications, television and movies today, I see more depictions of what I look like. When I looked in the mirror, all I saw was a person yearning to be someone else, to look like someone else. Weight was introduced to me at a young age and I was constantly reminded. Being 14 years old and feeling uncomfortable around your family because they may not eat as much as you is not fun. Or going in a store and trying on clothes and a family member or friend makes a scene about your having to have a bigger size than they have. I thought I was ugly and that is the point of it all. I felt unattractive and that permeated through my pores and my soul. I remember Lauryn Hill gracing the May 1999 issue of *Ebony Magazine*, and it was at that moment that I began to consider the beauty in the fullness of my lips, as hers were portrayed so beautifully. But who taught me to hate myself? People have a habit of speaking death when they believe they are being encouraging. The death that was spoken to me pierced every part of my self-esteem throughout my life to the point that when I looked in the mirror I saw nothing, at least nothing that I wanted to see. But God… God is so intentional and has a way of forcing his presence whether we want to acknowledge it or not; he is omniscient, omnipresent, and omnipotent.

I am, because of love. Love from teachers, family, friends, and others who have mentored me and molded me into the person that I continue to become. I knew early that I wanted to be a woman of integrity, respect, and love. To all the many women who have modeled this for me, thank you. Sometimes I think that I chose some wonderful women to mentor me, but then I'm not so sure if I chose them or if they were placed in my life through divine intervention. And to that point, I thank those women for fulfilling their purpose in my life. So, I say to the one reading my words:

- Who have you seen that you admire or would like to be mentored by?

_____
_____
_____
_____
_____
_____
_____
_____
_____
_____
_____
_____
_____
_____

- Who inspires you, encourages you, believes in you, trusts you and loves you?

_____
_____
_____
_____
_____
_____
_____
_____

- Who do you feel you can learn from?

_____
_____
_____
_____
_____
_____
_____
_____

Bold Love: A Letter To My Young Sisters

One thing that black women have grown away from is supporting, loving, encouraging and being genuine to one another. Who taught us that? Why did we let a divide come between us, and most importantly how can we be restored? "The most disrespected person in America is the black woman. The most unprotected person in America is the black woman. The most neglected person in America is the black woman," (Malcolm X, 1962) and a lot of the hate comes from within our own circles. What harm is it in offering another black woman a compliment, or wanting to join talents with her? Black women are worthy of the same wealth, promotion, and success as anyone else, but if we don't believe it and stop stepping on our sisters, our community will continue to be erased and will continue to be forced to assimilate into the main culture. The funny thing is other minority races build their own communities, create jobs for one another and grow and build off of other races. Blacks, however, believe we have arrived because we are no longer in the back of the bus. Reality is, we're only two seats up so the fight must still go on.

Melanin Me

By Terri M. Bolds

Oh that cocoa brown, caramel coated with cream sprinkled with dark richness

Skin pure and tight, smooth and sometimes rough, and well you know, feels so right

Kissed by sun approved by the creator

Loved by some, envied by others, and hated by…

Well what can I do about the fact that the melanin me is seen as inferior or intimidating?

How come I have to use less of my mind and vocabulary because I have been kissed by the sun and

Approved by God and then I wonder

Why does she and she, her and her and you and you that are shades of me seem to well…

Dis me too? I'm so confused by the melanin me

But I decided the melanin me is me

Bold Love: A Letter To My Young Sisters

The spirit that dwells in me is allowed to breed warmth, love and create good things

Cocoa brown, caramel coated with cream sprinkles with dark richness, love the melanin that is we

'Cause you see, we are queens, queens that need to keep climbing and not falling prey to what

They think the melanin that you, that is me, should be

The melanin in you, in me, in we, provides protection, adds a special touch of beauty that some wish they could be

But to them, love that which is you, and to you, love the melanin that is you, that is me, that is we.

CONCLUSION

So, black girl, as I close my letter to you, I want to leave you with these final thoughts. Be unapologetically yourself. We are living in a society where you can mask yourself behind technology and other ideas that diminish your true self. Whoever you are, be that. Blacks have been systematically groomed to hate ourselves. Cultural appropriation started with the field slave wanting to look like the misses in the big house or have skin as fair as the house slave or "good hair" that could braid and hang like a smooth neat rope. As time passed, blacks began to appreciate their blackness; however some still lingered in the "field" mindset. It is that mindset that has suppressed the genuine esteem we could have for ourselves. Instead, we are constantly fighting for acceptance.

Embrace who you are. You were created with a purpose. That purpose is not to feel inferior or be fearful of whom you were created to be: a black girl. You come from an ancestry of strength, power, faith, and intelligence. You are a branch on a tree of richness that helped build this country. You are the descendant of African royalty. Stuff happens, that seemingly deviates from the plan God has set for our lives. When this happens, it is not a green light for self-degradation, rather the pass for you to use the resilience that flows through your veins in order to navigate the new path presented before you. You don't have to defile your body with promiscuous behavior in order to suppress the years of sexual abuse you endured, or to seek the love you were never given, or to be accepted in circles that you believe to be "all the rave." You do not have to alter your body parts because you feel like that wand of God's touch in your maturation was flawed. You don't have to create scenarios that put you in the limelight because you feel like being smart and morally based are unpopular. You don't have to live with a tortured mind, saturating your pillow with tears of pain from the holes in your spirit. You don't have to date outside of your race because of the notion that black women are too direct and bossy. You don't have to do yourself harm, crying out for control and expressing emotion due to lack of self-worth because of events that happened to you that were not your fault. If you come from the projects, low-income housing, a single-parent home, an unconventional family, embrace that which is you!

Although I graduated in the top 10% of my high school class, received a few scholarships, received my bachelor's degree, master's degree, and was a licensed therapist all by the time I was 24, it took me until my thirties to start appreciating who I was created to be and who I turned out to be. When I looked in the mirror sometimes I wondered why I was so dark, why I had to have such strong ethnic features, why my hair was not longer. Why, why, why, why? What I should have been saying was, "Our deepest fear is not that we are inadequate. Our deepest fear is that we are powerful beyond measure. It is our light, not our darkness that most frightens us. We ask ourselves, who am I to be brilliant, gorgeous, talented, and fabulous? Actually, who are you not to be? You are a child of God. Your playing small does not serve the world. There is nothing enlightened about shrinking so that other people won't feel insecure around you. We are all meant to shine, as children do. We were born to make manifest the glory of God that is within us. It's not just in some of us; it's in everyone. And as we let our own light shine, we unconsciously give other people permission to do the same. As we are liberated from our own fear, our presence automatically liberates others" (Williamson, 1992).

 If you don't love yourself, no one else will fill that void. Not loving yourself can create a pattern of unhealthy relationships and have an adverse effect on what your life was created to be. Unfortunately, being black is not always glamorous, so make sure you don't need a fanfare in those times. Understand that although we are not still sitting in the back of the bus, we are only two seats up. We have not arrived to a place where there is equality for those considered a minority. So, when it is unpopular to be a black girl, carry the confidence that it does not matter whether the headline reads "Black Girls Rock" or "All Girls

Bold Love: A Letter To My Young Sisters

Rock." The key to having a healthy self-esteem is being honest and confident. Be honest with what you struggle with and what comes easy. Be honest about your hurts and how they have crippled you, and be confident in your ability to live beyond your past. Loving yourself as a black woman does not discount the beauty of all women.

Black people have been stigmatized with the untrue affiliation with always playing the race card and creating segregation. Black platforms were created as a result of the absence of diversity. Hip Hop was created to tell the story of the black individual. Braids and afros are an aesthetic part of our culture that displays diversity. Thick thighs and full-lips are the beautiful attributes that the creator saw fit to give the black race. Be confident in that. Learn and love your heritage. Black girls, live life with the paradoxical notion that while black supposedly isn't beautiful, others pay to acquire the physical qualities that we naturally possess because those things are acceptable as long as they are not on a black girl. These are the paradigms that generationally suppress our culture and we blindly allow it to occur.

So, black girl, live in your purpose without fear and self-hate. Don't focus on fighting for rites of passage; simply live in your "dopeness." Walk with your head held high enough to stand eye-to-eye with anyone, but low enough to never forget that humility reigns over conceit. Your skin, no matter how dark or how light, how ashy or how scarred; your hair, no matter how short or long, course and kinky or smooth and curly, is who you are and you need you to love yourself.

Terri M. Bolds, MS, LPC

My letter to you is a letter to my younger self, my now self and future self. "You are worthy, because you're here" (Oprah Winfrey).

Terri M. Bolds, MS, LPC

Steady fire. Some bright flames flicker and then die out. The light Terri Bolds brings with her Bold Visions will burn bright for many years to come.

Growing up in the urban districts of the Cincinnati Public School System, Terri was inspired to create an environment that will allow adolescents to find a place to help shape their own future.

Currently, serving as a Clinical Advisor, Terri's role ranges from providing consultation on crisis support for individual clients to coordinating support for intensive case management like conducting comprehensive professional assessments for substance abuse, domestic violence, and other trauma-related incidents.

Terri has served her community as group facilitator, adolescent therapist, and adjunct professor for a number of local colleges in the Cincinnati area. She has also had an article published in a National Magazine.

Combining her skill-sets as a Licensed Professional Counselor and a passion for youth and education, Terri endeavors to open her own facility to serve the needs of her broader community bringing mental, physical, and spiritual healing to a hurting population.

Terri is a survivor of her own trauma growing up as a young girl in Cincinnati and she has created a safe place for other survivors who need a place to start the healing process.

Terri Bolds is the founder of Bold Visions Consulting, a consulting business that serves the community through facilitating workshops, service projects and teaching classes about mental health with an emphasis on self-esteem and self-empowerment.

www.ingramcontent.com/pod-product-compliance
Lightning Source LLC
Chambersburg PA
CBHW052118070526
44584CB00017B/2549